IMAGES
of America

ATTLEBORO

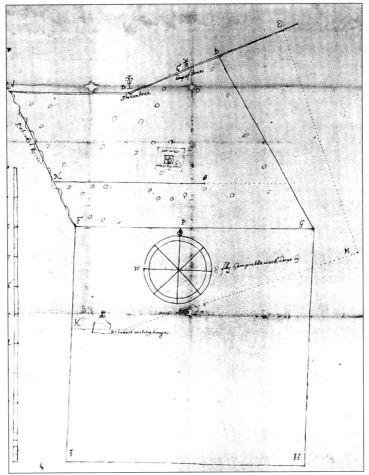

COPY OF THE OLDEST MAP OF ATTLEBOROUGH. On February 27, 1694, the "Great and Generall Court or Assemble" held at Boston appointed a committee to view the line between the Town of Rehoboth and the North Purchase or the Town of Attleborough. A strip of land, 1.5 miles wide had been claimed by both towns since 1666. The map shows the location of the Minister's 100 acres (now Old Town), and the Rehoboth Meeting House. Also located is the "Station Tree" site later to be called the Angle Tree Stone. It was not until 1710 that the claims were finally settled and the land was given to the Town of Attleborough. (AHC.)

IMAGES
of America

ATTLEBORO

Victor Bonneville
and Paula T. Sollitto

ARCADIA

Published by Arcadia Publishing,
an imprint of Tempus Publishing, Inc.
2 Cumberland Street
Charleston, SC 29401

Printed in Great Britain.

Library of Congress Catalog Card Number: 99-62399

For all general information contact Arcadia Publishing at:
Telephone 843-853-2070
Fax 843-853-0044
E-Mail arcadia@charleston.net

For customer service and orders:
Toll-Free 1-888-313-BOOK

Visit us on the internet at http://www.arcadiaimages.com

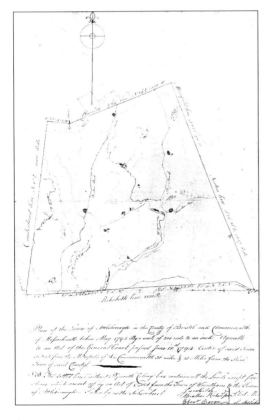

ATTLEBOROUGH, 1795. According to the caption on this map, the "Plan of the Town of Attleborough in the County of Bristol and Commonwealth of Massachusetts taken May 1795. . . agreeable to an Act of the General Court passed June 18, 1794. Center of said town Scituate from the Metropolis of this Commonwealth 36 miles and 15 miles from the Shire Town of said County. –N.B. the dotted lines without Plymouth Colony contains all the lands except five acres which was set off by an Act of Court from the Town of Wrentham to the Town of Attleborough. Taken by us the subscribers—Jacob Ide, Abiathar Richardson, Ebenr Bacon—Select Men of Attleborough." (AHC.)

CONTENTS

Introduction   7

Dedication   8

1.   Leisure Time   9

2.   Serving and Services   23

3.   Schools   37

4.   In and Around   51

5.   Fire and Other Disasters   65

6.   Working and Earning   79

7.   Getting About   91

8.   Celebration and Ceremonies   109

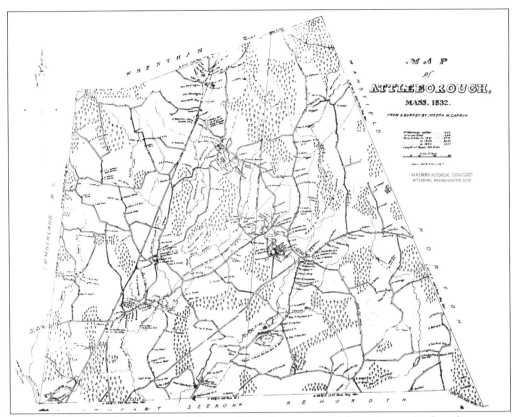

1832 MAP. In 1830, the General Court of the Commonwealth again required each town to make another plan. Joseph W. Capron of Attleborough, a civil engineer, was assigned to this town. The original map of 1831 is stored at the National Archives in Washington, D.C. In 1832, Mr. Capron made the map pictured above. (AHC.)

INTRODUCTION

Nothing endures but change.
–Heraclitus

Change is what Attleboro has been all about. This book will show some of these changes. One of the first changes for what would become Attleboro occurred in 1661 when, on April 8, Captain Thomas Willett, on behalf of some English settlers, purchased a large tract of land from Wamsutta, a chief of the Wampanoag Indians. Known as "The North Purchase," the land would be a part of Rehoboth for the next 33 years.

As the number of settlers increased, the North Purchase was incorporated into a new township, in 1694, by the Great and General Court of Massachusetts. As some of the settlers in the new township came from Attleborough, England, they, following a common practice throughout England's colonies, named their settlement "Attleborough." The newly created township would include present-day North Attleborough as well as Attleboro.

Religion played a major part in another change for Attleborough when, in 1743, the Congregational parish was split into two parishes—"First Parish" in the west of the town and "Second Parish" in the east. The seed for a future, permanent split between West Parish (North Attleborough) and East Parish (Attleboro) was thus sowed.

Change in transportation would also help to further this separation. Early transportation followed Native-American footpaths and trails, and as roads developed and became "highways," they were located primarily in the western part of Attleborough. However, when railroads began to increase in importance as transportation for both people and products to and from market, East Attleborough's location near this new, modern means of transportation would result in a rapid increase in both its population and industry, especially jewelry and related industries. In 1836, the main railroad line from Boston to Providence was built through the center of East Attleborough, thus placing the forces of the major change of 1887 in place.

The "S" word was probably used many times, at many town meetings, throughout these year, but the final separation ("S") of what was now being called "East Village" from "West Village" would not be done without much debate, concern, and soul searching by the people of Attleborough. Finally, in 1887, by a narrow margin, the town of Attleborough voted to separate into North Attleborough (West Village) and Attleborough (East Village). Now the people would deal separately with whatever changes the future might bring to their separated communities.

The change in spelling of Attleborough to Attleboro took place in 1914, when Attleborough received its city charter from the state legislature and became the City of Attleboro (a much more modern and dynamic spelling, which reflected the citizens' view of themselves and their community). Attleboro has continued to change ever since. We hope that this book, by giving us a look back at what Attleborough was, will prove to be a connection to what Attleboro is and what it might become.

This book is dedicated to the people of Attleboro, especially the children, past, present, and future, that they may know why Attleboro has been, is, and will be such a special place. Money earned from the sale of this book will be used to help fund the repair and maintenance of the Wolfenden Fountain at Capron Park.

One

LEISURE TIME

As so-called "leisure time" increased, with the transformation from an agricultural community to one of made up of many small shops and factories, how people spent their new-found free time became important. Attleboro would offer many ways for residents to spend their leisure time, including parks and playgrounds, clubs and social organizations, sports teams, school activities, and community celebrations of holidays and other special occasions.

BICENTENNIAL CELEBRATION, 1894. By carriage, bicycle, wagon, or foot, people came to celebrate Attleborough's 200th birthday. This is a scene is Park Street. The two-day celebration included dances, concerts, parades, and fireworks, which attracted more than 30,000 people. (APL.)

JOSEPH W. CAPRON, AGE 84. The Bicentennial celebration was so successful that 100 subscribers donated $2 each for a Tricentennial celebration in 1994. The first name on the list of subscribers was Joseph W. Capron. The $200 subscribed would grow over the 100 years to $20,000, which the City used to fund a huge fireworks display on October 19, 1994, at Hayward Field. (AHC.)

SOUVENIR PICTURE. This image was made at the time of the dedication of Capron Park on September 2, 1901. The Capron name is closely associated with celebrations and leisure-time activities. The park was given to the town by the children of Dennis Capron, as a memorial to his name. Capron Park remains a jewel in the city and attracts people from near and far. (AHC, donated by Mrs. E. Westcott.)

NEWELL SHELTER, C. 1912. Given by Mr. and Mrs. Frederich Newell at a cost of $5,000, the shelter was dedicated in 1910. Mr. Newell was a partner of Watson, Newell, and Co. (est. 1874), which produced sterling flatware and hollowware. Alas, Mr. Newell died before the structure was completed and his widow dedicated the building to his memory. (SC.)

NEWELL SHELTER, C. 1912. The town's annual report described the building as follows, "It sets back from County Street close to the pine grove, being fairly close to the bandstand and playground area. Its bright red (hip, tile) roof contrasts with the gray stone and green background and makes a beautiful as well as extremely useful addition to the park." Although the concrete shelter survived the Hurricane of 1938, the "pine grove" was destroyed. (SC.)

CAPRON PARK, C. 1912. The park provides a quiet place for leisure moments. A zoo, which has been added to the park, gives another reason to visit. (SC.)

FOOTPATHS AND BANDSTAND, CAPRON PARK, C. 1912. Whether one wished to take a quiet walk or attend a concert, the park provided for both. The tradition of band concerts on warm, summer evenings has continued to the present day. (SC.)

PLAYGROUND SWINGS AND SLIDE, CAPRON PARK, C. 1912. Swings, one of the more daring of playground equipment, are shown in motion here. Modern playgrounds deter children from attempting to go "over the bar;" safety concerns have made modern swings tame in comparison to earlier versions. (SC.)

SEESAW, CAPRON PARK, C. 1912. The play area may have changed to include more "modern" playground equipment, but it still remains one of the park's more appealing sites for family visits. (SC.)

ON THE RIVER. The rivers that run through Attleboro have not only been used for industrial purposes, but also have provided additional leisure-time opportunities. Jim Wallace's Canoe House, c. 1914, was located on Bank Street, east of the bridges, and provided canoe rentals. Jim Wallace is pictured standing at the right of the door with the bare arms. (SC.)

BANK STREET BRIDGE, 1914 OR EARLIER. Jim Wallace, on the extreme right, helps a young girl paddle along. Attempts to clean the 10 Mile, 7 Mile, and Bungay Rivers and the construction of the new river walkway suggests a return to the days when Attleboro enjoyed leisure use of its waterways. (SC.)

SOCCER TEAM, PERHAPS AT BRADY FIELD. Attleboro's many manufacturing companies provided various athletic diversions from the workplace. While the exact company sponsor is not certain here, the Wolfenden Company is believed to have been this team's backer. (SC.)

MCRAE'S AND KEELER'S BASEBALL TEAM. The most popular of early 1900s sports, company baseball teams would play in local leagues and against teams from the surrounding area. (SC.)

CYCLISTS AT WENDELL FARM, LOCUST STREET. Riding with friends was a popular pastime in Attleboro. Groups would often cycle from Attleboro to attend dances, picnics, and other social events. (SC.)

16

THE FINBERG ATHLETIC CLUB. Baseball players from various teams gathered here for this photograph. The father of former Attleboro Mayor Cyril K. Brennan is on the far right in the last row. (AHC.)

HUSTLERS. Baseball was not only for working adults; it was also for the young. While formal league may be how it's done today, encouraging the young to play and love the game has a long history. (AHC.)

BEATON'S NATIONAL BAND ON PARK STREET. Beaton is on the extreme right. According to John Laing Gibb (5/30/60), "Beaton had a professional band at the time Mr. Gibb came to Attleboro in 1902 as supervisor of music in the public schools. Beaton was a very fine bandmaster and wrote music. Beaton told Gibb that he shouldn't teach music in the schools as it would take bread out of the mouths of professional musicians. Nonetheless, Beaton sold the schools many instruments. Tom Hayward succeeded Beaton as Bandmaster around World War I." (SC.)

NORFOLK AND BRISTOL COUNTY STREET RAILROAD BAND, C. 1914. One of Attleboro's many different bands is shown here at the corner of Park and Pleasant Streets. The sign in the upper left-hand corner shows people's concern for painless dentistry. Some things don't change. (SC.)

19

MASQUERADE AT THE PILGRIM CHURCH (UNDATED). Various nations of the world are represented here in costume. Performers wore costumes form the Orient, Mexico, and the United States. (SC.)

OPEN AIR THEATER, TALAGUEGA PARK, 1902. Many streetcar companies attempted to add to the number of riders on these cars by building amusement parks for their passengers. Talaguega Park was opened on June 16, 1902. Two years later, a $75,000 casino was opened. In 1917, when trolley service began to decline, the park was sold, remodeled, and became the Bristol County Tuberculosis Hospital. (SC.)

HIGHLAND COUNTRY CLUB. Members of the city's country club could enjoy another popular leisure time activity — golf. Then, as now, the country club involved more than a game of golf. Parties, dances, dinners, and other social activities occupied club members. (AHC.)

BASEBALL GAME BETWEEN MARRIED AND SINGLE MEN, JULY 4, 1900. Shown here are, from left to right, Walter E. Briggs, Fred Alton, Ralph C. Estes, Ernest Bliss, Arno French, Dr. R.P. Dakin, Edward L. Gower, Aldro French, Ernest Lawton, Edward Fargo, Edward Anthony, and George Lilly. Social activities such as this would attract full attendance all day long on holidays. No one dared to leave town for fear they would miss out on an exciting time. (APL, *Highland 50 Year Booklet.*)

VIRTUE HOLMAN'S BIRTHDAY PARTY, C. 1902. Another thing that has not changed is having friends over to celebrate a birthday. Inez (Smith) Pearce is in the second row, third from left, and sister Grace (Smith) is in the same row, fifth from left. (APL.)

A SECONDARY SCHOOL PARTY. Miss Gow's Class, October 30, 1916, celebrates Halloween. The members of the class, shown here from left to right, are as follows: (front row) Marion Marshall; (middle row) Ruth Whipple, Gertrude Baker, Miss Gow, Gladys Johnson, Laura Hoddie, Viola Brachway, and Marion Power; (back row) Elsie Deladeo (fourth), and Althea Robinson (sixth). Others pictured are unidentified. (AHC.)

Two

SERVING AND SERVICES

Then, as now, mailmen, policemen, firemen, and servicemen and so many others (both men and women) provide the often taken-for-granted services of everyday life in the city. From its churches, library, hotels, service groups, to a clean and safe water supply, the city provides many services and many ways for its people to serve, making life easier for all who live in Attleboro.

RURAL CARRIER, JUNE 26, 1909. The delivery of mail is one of the services provided to people who eagerly await the phrase, "You've got mail." John T. Small, age 78, is pictured here as he pauses a moment on his appointed rounds. (AHC.)

ATTLEBORO MAIL CARRIERS, C. 1918. Seen here in the driveway of the Bates Block (note playbill on right), these mail carriers would soon be bringing cards and letters from friends and loved ones to people throughout the city. In 1820, East Attleborough would get its own postmaster, Ezra Bassett. (SC.)

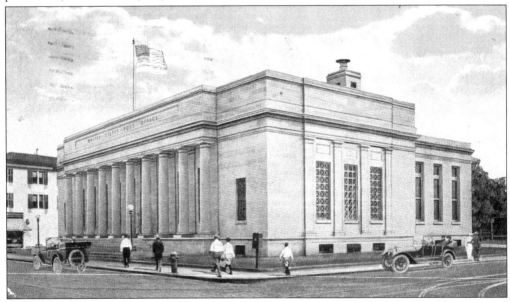

POST OFFICE BUILDING. As mail has changed in delivery, type, and definition, the once proud temple of mail service, which opened in 1917 at a cost of $125,000, has been abandoned by the U.S. Postal Service. Replaced by a new structure on the outskirts of the city, the mail still gets delivered. (AHC.)

ATTLEBORO POLICE FORCE (UNDATED). Attleboro has maintained a police department to help and protect its people. This early 1900s photograph shows the force in a quiet moment, but as the city has grown in population, so too has the size of its police department. (SC.)

OUTSIDE CITY JAIL. Constable (or Sheriff) John Nerney is shown with a prisoner outside the city's jail. John Nerney later set aside his police duties and started Nerney Motor Sales, the first automobile dealership in the city. (SC.)

"FIRE!" Another important service that the city provides is its fire department. Here, in an undated photograph, a horse-drawn hose engine is pictured en route to a fire in the Dodgeville section of the city. Since the city's buildings were mostly wooden structures, the fire department would be especially hard-pressed to stop fires once they had started. (SC.)

UNION STREET HOSE HOUSE. As the city's population grew, new demands for city services would require the building of more "hose" houses to serve the people. The Union Street Hose House was located close to the heart of Attleboro's rapidly growing jewelry industry. (AHC.)

IDE'S HILL STANDPIPE, ERECTED 1905–1906. As the town grew, its concern for providing an adequate supply of water prompted the construction of what was then the largest, freestanding concrete structure in America. (AHC and the Attleboro Public Works Department.)

THE ATTLEBORO SANITARIUM. Opened in 1902 at a cost of $400,000, the sanitarium attracted people in need of respite from an ever increasing, stress-filled world. Dr. James M. Solomon, who had the sanitarium built, claimed that because of his Native-American "medicine man" heritage, as well as his medical training and experience, he could guarantee the cure of cancer and tumors. The sanitarium, also known as the Soloman Sanitarium, closed at the end of 1937. Today it continues to serve as a respite, especially each Christmas season as the site of the Christmas Festival of Lights of LaSallete Shrine. (AHC.)

ATTLEBORO PUBLIC LIBRARY. While most cities and towns contain libraries, Attleboro's beautiful library building has a story that reflects the city's "can-do" character. As Andrew Carnegie worked to implement his "Gospel of Wealth" by providing money for the building and support of libraries throughout the United States, Attleboro was not a beneficiary of the great man's wealth. Undeterred, the sturdy citizens of Attleboro raised the necessary money locally, built its library, and in 1908, the new library was given to the town for the benefit of its residents. The cost totaled $85,000, over twice the original estimate of $37,000. (SC.)

OLD PECK HOUSE. Moved from its original site to its present location on the corner of Elizabeth and North Main Streets, the colonial house, one of the oldest in the city, now serves as the meeting house for the local chapter of the Daughters of the American Revolution (DAR). Marion Pierce Carter founded the DAR in Attleboro in 1902. Throughout the years, Attleboro has had many clubs and organizations that have given the city a rich tradition of service. (AHC.)

PIKE'S HOTEL, WINNECUNNETT. This Hotel, like many others, served the needs of weary travelers. Most, like Pike's Hotel, have disappeared from the urban landscape as transportation methods and locations have changed through the years. (SC.)

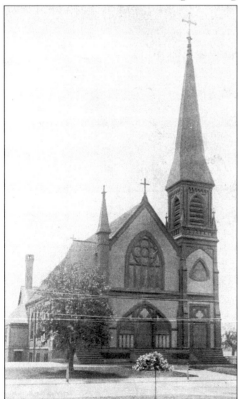

ST. JOHN THE EVANGELIST CHURCH. Dedicated on September 22, 1885, the church, located on North Main Street, helped serve the needs of Attleboro's growing Roman Catholic population. St. John was destroyed by fire on February 1, 1932. Cinders from its blaze, fanned by high winds, threatened to destroy the new parish church under construction nearby. Firemen were able to prevent the spread of the fire and the larger, grander Gothic-style church was dedicated on November 6, 1932. (AHC.)

REV. PETER THACHER. Exhibited in 1932 at the Robert C. Vose Galleries in Boston, this portrait of a descendant of Attleborough's Second Congregational Church's first pastor, Peter Thacher (1748–1785), was painted by Peter Pelham. Pelham taught John Singleton Copley how to draw and gave Copley his first lessons in painting. An attempt by George E. Nerney and other church members to raise enough money to purchase the portrait was not successful. (AHC.)

SECOND CONGREGATIONAL CHURCH. The "White Church" replaced the church's first meeting house, which had been built in 1748. With the North Baptist Church in Providence as its model, work was begun in the spring of 1825 on the new structure. The new church was dedicated in December of the same year. (AHC.)

WHITE CHURCH, PRE-1908. This winter scene shows the Old Park Street railroad crossing. Disregarding strong protests, the Boston and Providence Railroad laid its tracks through the Kirk Yard Cemetery near the church in 1833. Approximately 150 bodies had to be removed and re-buried nearby. (SC.)

WHITE CHURCH. An Attleboro landmark, the church's outward appearance changed little over the years. The White Church would stand side by side with the new brick church until it was torn down in 1954. (APL. Given by Mrs. Charles Mooers.)

OLD AND NEW CHURCH. As church membership grew, a new brick church was dedicated beside the White Church in May of 1904. The two church buildings would serve the congregation until the mid-1940s, when the White Church was finally closed. (APL.)

OFF TO SERVE, ATTLEBORO DEPOT, 1916. The city's military company is shown here, leaving Attleboro (probably on their way to Texas), as relations with Mexico grew more difficult. The large crowd wishes "God speed" to friends and relatives as the men of Company I answered the call to serve. (SC.)

COMPANY I IN TEXAS. Called into active service in June of 1916, the men are shown taking time out from their training and duties to pose for this photograph. The company served as part of Gen. John J. Pershing's Expeditionary force, which tried unsuccessfully to capture Pancho Villa. (SC.)

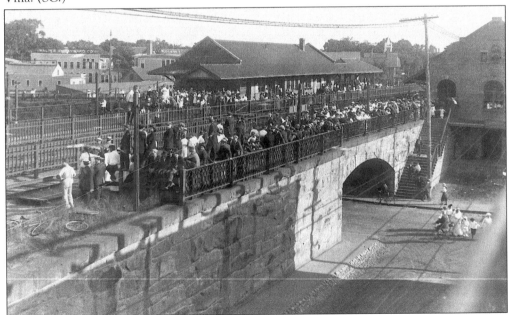

HOME AGAIN. Returning to Attleboro on November 15, 1916, the men of Company I would be greeted by their family and friends, shown here awaiting the men's return from Texas. Company I served along the Rio Grande at Clint and San Elizario, south of El Paso. (SC.)

COMPANY I IN DOWNTOWN ATTLEBORO. Organized in 1887, Company I voted to call itself the "Attleborough Light Infantry" in 1888. The company helped prevent looting in Attleborough following the Great Fire of May 17, 1898. It served a similar duty following the Hurricane of 1938. (SC.)

COMPANY I, C. 1912. Opened on December 7, 1910, after much debate, the armory would become "home" for Company I. Shown marching down Railroad Avenue, the company would turn left here to reach its armory on Union Street. (SC.)

COMPANY I, C. 1914 ON PARK STREET. The company would be involved in all of the nation's conflicts from the Spanish-American War, labor unrest in Lawrence, Massachusetts — where the men served without incident — to World War I and II. It also marched in countless parades and took part in numerous ceremonies and celebrations, including Attleborough's Bicentennial of 1894. (SC.)

SUPPORTING THE TROOPS. When war in Europe called citizens to serve their country, Attleboro responded with great enthusiasm both on the home front and "over there." Company I would be combined with other Massachusetts volunteers and serve in France from 1917 until 1919. Liberty Loan drives raised well over $5,500,000 for the war effort. (AHC.)

Three

SCHOOLS

From colonial times to the present, communities have been involved in the education of their children. Attleboro's schools have a long and proud tradition of providing a high-quality education for the city's children. From one-room schoolhouses to today's modern facilities, Attleboro has shown that it considers education to be of the greatest importance.

SCHOOL DISTRICT #8. Erected in 1867, School District #8 was located in what is now called South Attleboro, just beyond the Newell Burial Ground and before present-day May Street. Several of Attleborough's 20 school district buildings continue to be used as private homes. (SC.)

TEACHERS AND STUDENTS. Looking straight into the camera, this *c.* 1890s unidentified class of students and their teachers pose for a class picture. Note the bicycle and outhouse building on the left. (AHC.)

BISHOP STREET SCHOOL BARGE, JUNE 22, 1925. Getting to school, then as now, was part of many students' educational day. This photograph was taken, possibly on the last day of school, on Lindsey Street, near the location of Swanton's Furniture Co. The school barge's route included Lindsey Street, Richardson Avenue, Pike Avenue, and Bishop Street for school at Bliss School. Mr. Kellogg was the driver. (SC.)

SANFORD STREET SCHOOL V, 1902. The arrow is pointing to Grace Smith, who is seen exercising with her classmates. The role of schools has grown over the years from the 3 Rs to many other areas, including physical education. Since elementary schools had no gymnasiums, such classes were held outside, weather permitting. (AHC.)

GYMNASIUM, WILLETT SCHOOL, c. 1940s. "Bodies strong and muscles trim / Full of Vigor, Pep, and Vim / Trained and fit to run and swim / are developed in the gym" was a well-known rhyme at Willett School. When the school opened in 1943, it was the first elementary school to have its own gymnasium. A school booklet, from which this photograph is taken, went to parents and students to prepare them for a successful school experience. (APL. "Getting Ready for School" (GRFS) booklet.)

TIME OUT. "Little tired heads and hands must have quiet rest after the mid-morning lunch, that's the time that's best." Part of the young student's day included time for "resting." This photograph and rhyme for Willett School students shows "little tired heads" at rest. With the opening of Willett School, Attleboro was able to eliminate the use of three wooden buildings that lacked modern safety and sanitary features. (APL, GRFS.)

HEALTH FAIR, 1923. Attleboro schools did not ignore basic health concerns. This photograph shows a school's outdoor program promoting good health habits. (APL.)

LUNCH TIME. Kindergarten students at Willett School are pictured here enjoying a lunch break, *c.* 1940s. Willett School continues to serve the children of Attleboro as an elementary school. It was completely renovated in the early 1990s. (APL, GRFS.)

ATTLEBORO TEACHERS, JUNE 1913. Buildings are one thing, but successful education depends upon teachers. Teachers, shown here from left to right, are identified by their last names as follows: (front row) Cutting, Howland, Luther, Harney, and Trail; and (standing) Johnson, Crossman, Christin, Hutchinson, Bake, Williams, and Yarleton. Carrie Luther (Bertenshaw) would continue to teach in Attleboro at the Pleasant Street and Bliss Schools until the 1950s. (AHC.)

ATTLEBORO HIGH SCHOOL (AHS), 1896.
Built at a cost of $15,000, the building would
serve as Attleboro High School until 1914,
after which it continued to be used as a
grammar and vocational school until 1941.
Mr. Joseph Osmond Tiffany was the principal
when the school opened with 34 students. On
the faculty was Miss Helen Metcalf, an English
teacher whose name lives on with the
presentation each year of scholarship prizes to
deserving graduating students. When Willett
School opened, the building was deemed
unnecessary and Mayor John W. McIntyre
ordered it razed. (APL.)

AHS BASEBALL TEAM, BEFORE 1902. Shown here, from left to right, are as follows: (front row)
Bob Witherell, Ambrose Warren (teacher), Norval Lamb, Albert Austin (teacher), and George
Roberts; (back row) unidentified, Lester Moore, Harold Richardson, Wilfred Rounseville,
unidentified, and Walter Cobb. (AHC. Given by Mrs. Robert Witherell.)

AHS FOOTBALL TEAM, 1902. Baseball and football were the sports for AHS athletes at the turn of the century. With the separation of the town in 1887, a strong sports rivalry developed between North Attleborough and Attleboro, which continues today. In 1921, the first AHS-North Thanksgiving Day football game was held, inaugurating one of the oldest such rivalries in Massachusetts. (APL.)

AHS FOOTBALL TEAM, BEFORE 1902. Seen here, from left to right, are as follows: (first row) Walter Cobb; (second row) Norval Lamb, Bob Wetherell, Walter E. Briggs, ? Gilmore, and Vernon White; (third row) Bill Roberts, Albert Austin (teacher), Ray Wells, ? Cooney, Wilfred Rounseville, and Frank Guild; (fourth row) John Evans, ? Torrey, George Nerney, Ralph Reed, and Lester Moore. (AHC. Given by Mrs. Robert Wetherell.)

AHS, BANK STREET SCHOOL. Pictured are students and faculty at the Bank Street School. The exact date is unknown. (AHC.)

FRESHMEN! The class of 1912 poses outside the Bank Street High School on June 15, 1909. (AHC.) This location would be used as the place where class pictures would be taken. Class photos were taken each year of the students' high school years.

GRADUATION. Grace Smith Miner is the tallest in this graduation photograph. The class was probably an eighth grade class at the Sanford Street School. Eighth-grade graduation was considered an important milestone in a young person's life. The Sanford Street School was named for Nathaniel W. Sanford, who gave the land to the town. (APL.)

AHS, 1909. This photograph was probably taken at the Bank Street High School. Graduation from high school was often not only a proud achievement; it also marked the end of formal schooling for many graduates. Attleboro's growing number of shops and factories would provide jobs for many after high school. (SC.)

AHS, 1910. With white tops and caps, this 1910 photograph continues an apparent tradition at Attleboro High School. Grace Smith is in the third row, fourth from the left. (AHC.)

GRADUATION RECEPTION. When the high school was located at Bank and Peck Streets, graduations were always held at the Bates Theater, which is the probable location of this photograph. (AHC.)

BUILDING THE "NEW" HIGH SCHOOL, C. 1912. As the city's population grew, the number of children grew also, and the need for a new high school became necessary. The next two photographs show the high school under construction. This view is looking south down County Street. (SC.)

BUILDING THE "NEW" HIGH SCHOOL, C. 1912. The new high school would include a gymnasium, which is shown here under construction. However, the "new" high school lacked space for outdoor sports, which necessitated the use of facilities away from the County Street site. Baseball and football home games were played at Hayward Field on North Avenue. The bleachers for the field were built in the back yard of the County Street high school, transported to the field, and assembled by AHS shop students under the supervision of George I. Spatcher, Faculty Manager of Athletics, who taught what was called "manual training" at the high school. (SC.)

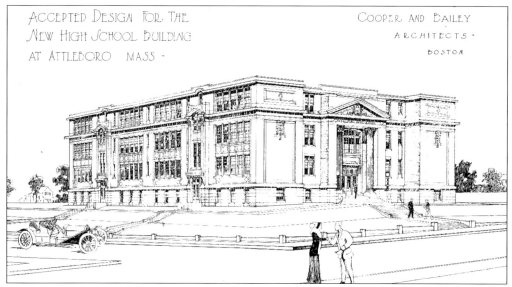

AHS. Still in use by the school department, the building on County Street was Attleboro's High School from 1914 until 1962, when it became the Cyril K. Brennan Junior High School. It would be a junior high school/middle school until 1998, when Brennan Middle School would be moved into a new building. (APL.)

GRADUATION 1917. The new County Street High School contained a large auditorium, which made possible a city-wide, eighth-grade graduation ceremony as seen here. Once again, the front entrance steps of the new building would be used as "the spot" for class pictures. (AHC.)

AHS BAND. Pictured here, on the front entrance, steps is John Laing Gibb and the AHS Band. Mr. Gibb became a music teacher in 1902, and for the next 40 years, he would further the idea of including music instruction as part of the school curriculum. Old-time professional bandmasters and musicians were originally opposed to Gibb's efforts, fearing that it would undermine their status and livelihood. (AHC.)

Four

IN AND AROUND

Streets, buildings, special places, these and more fill our mental picture of "Attleboro." Here are some of these sights in and around the city.

BATES BLOCK. Long the centerpiece of "Downtown Attleboro," located at the intersection of North and South Main Streets and County and Park Streets, the building shown here would serve the entertainment needs of the city by providing everything from live theater performances to movies. (SC.)

FARMING DAY. Like most New England communities, Attleborough began as a farming community. Although former farmers' fields have given way to manufacturing, housing, and other urbanization uses, there still are fields and woods that the city and many of its citizens are attempting to keep as special places in the urban landscape. (AHC.)

AUTUMN, 1900. The Attleborough landscape remains rural in this turn-of-the-century photograph. (AHC.)

"VIEW FROM 'MECHANICS.'" Tree-lined streets would dominate the community's landscape well into the 20th century. (AHC.)

OLD HOUSE (WEST ATTLEBORO), 389 NEWPORT AVENUE. Located near the Newell Burial Grounds in what is today called South Attleboro, this house is one of the city's oldest. A militia training ground was located nearby in colonial days. (AHC.)

SNOW! Was it colder then? Did it snow more often? Were the snow banks higher? This 1880s snow scene of Upper Holman Street reminds us of the beauty that exists following a snowstorm. (SC.)

DRIVING ON SNOW. The view shows Upper South Main Street, near the office of Dr. Holden from Herrick's Corner, *c.* 1880s. (SC.)

AFTER THE STORM. This view of Upper County Street was photographed from Herrick's Corner c. 1890s. (SC.)

COUNTY STREET. With trolley tracks visible on the right, County Street has long been one of Attleboro's main streets. (AHC.)

STATELY HOMES. Leading citizens and industrialists built their homes on County Street. As more people moved to East Attleborough, those who could began to seek more tranquil places to live. Near enough to Attleborough's growing number of industries to oversee local businesses, yet away from the bustle of the town's center, County Street proved to be an ideal location for many to build their new homes. The Wolfenden houses at 167 and 173 County Street are examples of such ideal locations. (AHC.)

THE OLD CAR. Trolley cars began to fade as the popular means of transportation and soon became mere curiosities. Photographed at at Albert Nickerson's, this car is filled with playful children. (SC.)

BATTLE OF PLEASANT STREET. As the trolleys faded and the auto gained popularity, the need to widen and improve streets became necessary. Progress, for some, often means disruption for others. The Cooper family "raised strenuous objections to the widening of Pleasant Street; (and) picketed the construction site carrying flags and Civil War muskets." (Mr. Doty, photographer; SC.)

STREET SCENE, NORTH MAIN. Still one of the more picturesque streets leading to Attleboro, North Main Street is pictured here, looking north from the Town Center. The steeple on the left is probably that of the first St. John the Evangelist Church.

SOUTH MAIN STREET CROSSING. It was the railroad that provided the engine for Attleboro's growth and development. Pictured here, at the corner of Mill and South Main Streets, looking north towards the Second Congregational Churches, are the tracks on which Attleboro products were transported by train to the larger markets of Boston, Providence, and New York City. (AHC; CKB)

THE CENTER. Tracks crisscross the downtown center of Attleboro on Park Street, looking west at the Bronson Building. (AHC; CKB.)

RAILROAD CROSSING. One of Attleboro's numerous lumber companies, Pierce & Carpenter Lumber Co., is pictured here on South Main Street, opposite Capron Street, looking north. AHC; CKB)

RAILROAD DEPOT. Horse-drawn vehicles are mixed with newer means of transportation in this *c.* 1912 scene. Capron's Garage is on the right. (SC.)

ATTLEBOROUGH'S ARCHES, C. 1910. The corner of Bank and Park Streets offers a splendid viewing point of Attleboro's railroad arches, built to elevate the railroad's passage through the growing center. The lovely, horse-drawn wagon appears to symbolize the passing of an era. (SC.)

PARK STREET, DOWNTOWN, 1920. Trolley tracks and autos mix in the flag-lined street, giving this city scene a sense of energy. (SC.)

BRONSON BUILDING. One of the cornerstones of the downtown area, this building offered space for businesses and offices. (SC.)

PARK HOTEL. This hotel on Park Street was a longtime fixture in Attleboro. (AHC. Donor: Mrs. E. Westcott.)

PARK HOTEL. A horse stable in the back of the hotel gave travelers a convenient place to keep their horses. Bicycles make their appearances here as another means of getting around. (SC.)

AFTER THE STORM. This view shows the Horton Building on the corner of Railroad and Park Streets. (SC.)

COUNTY STREET FROM THE BUSHEE BUILDING (BALFOUR), UNDATED. In this early view, trolley tracks line one side of the street and cars are parked along the other side. (SC.)

BATES THEATER. The theater may be gone, as in-town theaters have moved to multi-screen movie theaters near the malls and highways, but this building and some of the businesses shown here still remain. (SC.)

Five

FIRE AND OTHER DISASTERS

From natural disasters caused by wind or snow, to man-encouraged ones of fire, Attleboro has had its share of such tragedies. Not only did fire destroy factories and other manufacturing buildings, it also destroyed much of Attleboro's business district. The city, however, has always survived these disasters, rebuilt, and continued to grow and prosper.

THE GREAT FIRE OF '98. A hint of the Great Fire of May 17, 1898's destructive force is seen here. The photograph was used as the cover for a souvenir booklet of Attleboro that was published after the fire. The booklet shows Attleboro to be a prosperous town of fine homes and many factories despite the fire's recent destruction. (AHC.)

FIRE OF '98. As the midnight train from Providence, Rhode Island, arrived in Attleborough, some of its passengers became the first to see a fire burning in the basement of the Joseph M. Bates Factory, one of many jewelry factories located on the east side of the town along Mill Street. Once off the train, some of the passengers rushed to where they thought they had seen a fire and found the basement shop of J.T. Inman & Co. ablaze. It was the beginning of what would be the "Great Fire of '98." (SC.)

FIRE OF '98. Row after row of wooden, multi-story factory buildings, built only a few feet from one another, had floors soaked with oil and other chemicals as well as open rooms with work benches that spanned the entire length of the buildings. Without fire walls or other fire-retarding features, these buildings provided the ingredients for a disaster. (SC.)

FACTORY RUINS. The Fire of '98 destroyed 19 factories. While most of these factories were rebuilt, the fire caused some 3,000 workers to go jobless. The fire led to a $2-million building boom as manufacturers quickly rebuilt, this time with concern for safety. (SC.)

FIRE OF '98. Even before the fire had been completely extinguished, curious onlookers gathered to see the devastation it had caused. During the height of the fire, thousands came to watch. After the fire, martial law was declared to prevent the possible loss of gold, which was located in the ruins. (SC.)

FIRE OF '98. Attleboro Fire Chief Hiram R. Packard and men from the Hose and Ladder House No. 2, which was located on the corner of Union and Dunham Streets, were the first to respond to the alarm sent by night watchman John Berraine. Other alarms would soon be sounded as the need for more men and hoses became obvious. (SC.)

FIRE OF '98. The wind was another ingredient added to the mix of factors which led to this disaster. As window panes broke, the wind blew into the buildings, fueling the flames and sending sparks hundred of feet into the night sky. The wind would continue to add to the nightmare until it stopped abruptly at 2:20 a.m. The firemen then had a chance to stop the fire's spread and contain the blaze. (SC.)

FACTORY RUINS. Selectmen Chairman W.H. Goff telegraphed Pawtucket, Providence, and Taunton for help. North Attleborough's Hose 2 Co. from Attleboro Falls had arrived to help 25 minutes after it had been called. (SC.)

FIRE OF 1898. As Attleborough rebuilt, factories would be built farther apart from one another, and the town would begin to implement fire and building codes. The lessons learned from the Great Fire of '98 paved the way for safer work places. (SC.)

FIRE, 1912. This photograph probably shows the start of the Watson Building fire. This view is looking up County Street, with the Bates Block in front and the Bronson Building on the left. (SC.)

WATSON BUILDING FIRE, OCTOBER 29, 1912. Horses stand and wait as firemen battle the blaze. (SC.)

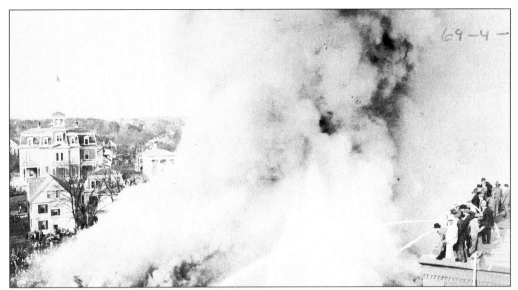

FIRE OF 1912. Other buildings provided a platform for firemen to fight the fire. (AHC. Donor: Mrs. E. Westcott.)

DOING BATTLE. This photo and the two on the page 72 show firemen atop the burning building as spectators line the street. (SC.)

71

DOING BATTLE II. Spectators watch as firemen work to contain the blaze. (SC.)

AFTER THE BATTLE. The ruins of the Watson Building can be seen here. (SC.)

HERRICK'S CORNER. At the corner of County, Park North, and South Main Streets, the jeweler and optician George H. Herrick's business gave its name to this downtown location. (AHC, gift of Henry Pelletier.)

HERRICK CORNER FIRE, 1917. People look at all that remained of the once proud jewelry shop. (SC.)

HERRICK'S CORNER FIRE. The fire would not only consume the corner, but Horton, Pierce, and Sanford Blocks would also be destroyed. Before the fire's fury was spent, its intensity heavily damaged the Bates, Monroe, Gifford, Sturdy, and Brownell blocks. (SC.)

HERRICK'S CORNER FIRE. Looking up Park Street, the Bronson Building is straight ahead, behind the streetcar. Most of the properties along Park Street in the downtown area suffered damage. (SC.)

AFTERMATH. This rare view of the Herrick's Corner Fire shows the F.W. Woolworth five and dime store, along with the Columbia Theater on Bank Street. Buildings on Union and Pine Streets were also damaged. (SC.)

1938 HURRICANE. One of the great storms to hit Attleboro was the no-name hurricane of 1938, which struck the area at 3 p.m., with little advance warning. Local photographer Frank E. Adams photographed the devastation. The following pictures are from his booklet "Where the 1938 Hurricane Struck in Attleboro," which is located both in the Attleboro Historical Commission and the Attleboro Public Library. Pictured here is the "first tree to fall in Attleboro. A large elm, it was located near the home of ex-mayor Stephen H. Foley, South Main Street." That's Dr. Anderson Briggs's car under the elm. (APL, *Booklet of '38 Hurricane* by Frank E. Adams.)

FLATTENED. This view of "the Common" shows the city's Veteran's Honor Roll as well as trees which were felled by the force of the storm. (APL, *Booklet of '38 Hurricane* by Frank E. Adams.)

UNINVITED COMPANY. John Gaboury's house on Cumberland Avenue, South Attleboro, had an unexpected visitor when this tree fell upon the house. Damage in the city was estimated at $5 million. (APL, *Booklet of '38 Hurricane* by Frank E. Adams.)

DEAN STREET. Trees were not the only victim of the '38 Hurricane. Here, a telephone pole has crashed into this Dean Street piazza. Power was lost throughout the city. (APL, *Booklet of '38 Hurricane* by Frank E. Adams.)

DEAN STREET. Looking toward North Main Street, Dean Street looked like this from one end to the other. The storm was also responsible for ten injuries. (APL.)

Six

WORKING AND EARNING

Attleboro has always been a working place, with jobs for its ever growing and changing population. Be it the jewelry industry or other related or unrelated businesses, Attleboro used its rivers and location along major transportation routes to develop its strong economic base.

"COME ONE, COME ALL." Then, as now, Attleboro worked hard to attract business and industry to the city. This WW I (c. 1918) vintage sign was located at the Attleboro Depot and boasted the city's appeal for new industry. (SC.)

THE BEGINNING. Founded by Mr. Fitzsimmons, shown here in the buggy with his secretary, the R.F. Simmons company would be one of Attleboro's great industries until 1962. Fitzsimmons dropped the "Fitz" when naming his company. These next four pictures are from murals painted by Percy Ball, and were located in the company's office building. (AHC.)

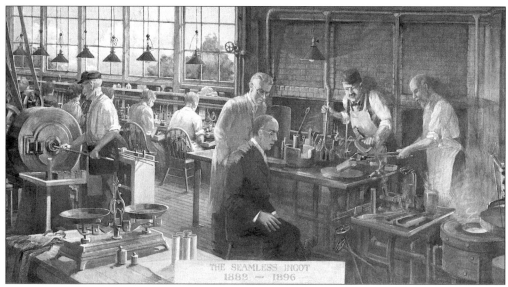

THE SEAMLESS INGOT, 1882–1896. Partner of the firm J.L. Sweet (seated) and Mr. Bluementhal (standing) are pictured at work at R.F. Simmons. The company had offices in New York City, as did many other Attleborough firms, but R.F. Simmons was so successful that it was also "represented" overseas in such cities as Rio de Janeiro, Buenos Aires, Berlin, Barcelona, and Sydney. (AHC.)

THE NEW SHOP, 1892. R.F. Simmons' "new shop" was conveniently located near the Bungay R., with the railway stopping just outside. At this time, it was one of the town's largest employers and would remain so for many years. (AHC.)

NEW YORK CITY. R.F. Simmons was a large supplier of railroad conductors' chains. Here conductors are shown in a New York City store picking out their chains. The company's success was based on its well-deserved reputation for high quality products. (AHC.)

R.F. Simmons. Purchased in 1962 by Josten's Inc., the once proud Attleboro factory would soon close and the building would eventually be torn down. (SC.)

Also Gone. The James E. Blake Factory on South Main Street, shown here in a pre-WW I photograph, would house many small jewelry or jewelry-related companies over the years. Women dressed in white are seen with parasols as protection from the sun. This building would also fall victim to change and be demolished in the 1990s. (SC.)

JEWELERS' SUPPLIES. Charles Thurber and John Evans look out the door of George L. Claflin Co. on Union Street as a wagon, loaded with supplies for local jewelry firms, is set to make its deliveries. (SC.)

PINE STREET, C. 1906–1910. Attleboro's factory buildings often housed many different types of companies within the same building. This Pine Street building contained pattern photographer, Bay State Optical Co., and another jewelry firm. (SC.)

PINE AND DUNHAM STREETS. A horse and wagon patiently wait while being loaded outside the C.H. Allen and Co. (SC.)

UNION AND MILL STREETS. Founded in 1882, the D.F. Briggs Co. shared this building with other manufacturing firms. (SC.)

FRANK MOSSBURG COMPANY, FOUNDED 1898. The company was located on the corner of South Main and Mill Streets and Railroad Avenue. Born in Sweden, Frank Mossburg would become an inventor, businessman, and civic leader in Attleboro. In the early 1900s, his company attracted other Swedish immigrants to Attleboro who would provide much of the skilled labor for Mossburg's company. (SC.)

CONNECTED. Surrounding communities were also tied to Attleboro's booming industries by roads and trolley. Pictured here is the Copper Works in nearby Norton. (SC.)

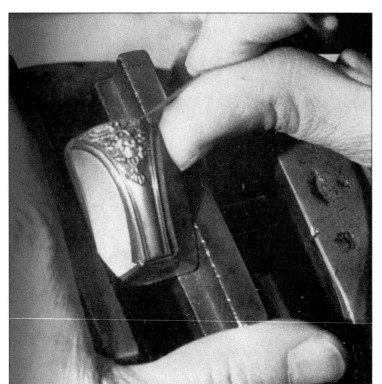

L.G. BALFOUR COMPANY. For much of the 20th century, the L.G. Balfour Co. would be Attleboro's leading jewelry firm. As shown in the following photographs from *The Balfour Story*, skilled craftsmen produced the rings and other items for which the company became famous. (AHC.)

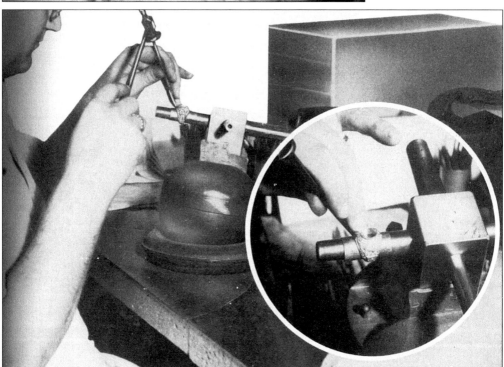

SKILLED HANDS. From class rings to team championship rings, L.G. Balfour would come to dominate the field of achievement recognition in America. (*The Balfour Story*, AHC.)

MADE IN ATTLEBORO. Customers ranged from the U.S. Government to large and small companies as well as colleges and high schools. (*The Balfour Story*, AHC)

D.H. CAPRON'S LIVERY STABLE, 1880S. Work was not only available in Attleboro factories, but also in other businesses needed by the community. Located on Park Street and Railroad Avenue, D.H. Capron's Livery Stable provided for the needs of Attleboro's horses and other animals. (SC.)

OLD SAWMILL. As Attleboro grew, wood for homes and factories was in great demand. This sawmill, probably on Tiffany Street, would help supply such products. (SC.)

Left: TOM ROBBINS AND A WAITRESS. Feeding Attleboro's large working population would also help to create more jobs for waitresses, cooks, and many others. (SC). *Right.* WATER TANKS AND CHIMNEY. Bushee Factory, off County Street was built in 1872. The completion of the three-story wooden structure would see the rapid growth of the firm, which would specialize in "separable cuff and collar buttons." With an office in New York City, the Bushee brothers, Albert A. and Charles H., would become one of Attleborough's early jewelry company success stories. (SC.)

OLD TIME MILK WAGON. Home delivery! W.H. Smith and a helper are shown here in Hebronville, about to set off on their appointed rounds. (SC.)

OLD TIME COUNTY STREET. Many early industries were located along, or near, County Street. Many "factory buildings," such as the one pictured here, contained numerous companies within the same building. (SC.)

DINERS. Diners provided workers with quick, inexpensive, and tasty meals during their lunch breaks. Here is Bill Muloney's diner, which was located on South Main Street looking toward Park Street. (SC.)

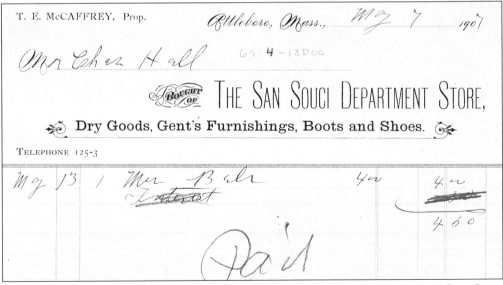

SAN SOUCI'S. In the early 1900s, Attleboro's leading department store was San Souci Department Store. Located on South Main Street, near the city's many factories, it would be destroyed by fire in 1917. (AHC, Donor: Mrs. E. Westcott.)

Seven
GETTING ABOUT

Besides providing a place to live and work, successful communities need to provide good access into and out of the city as well as within city limits. This chapter will show Attleboro's many methods for "getting about."

DANGER AHEAD. Until the invention of the automobile, dirt streets were the norm in American cities. This photograph from a department of public works album shows work being done to upgrade Railroad Avenue in 1921. (DPW Album, AHC.)

WATERING PLACE ON COUNTY ROAD AND MR. THOMAS S. CARPENTER. Streets would often be shared not only with people, horses, and horse-drawn carriages, but also with cattle as all moved about in Attleborough's early agricultural days. (AHC.)

GOING TO WORK? Above is a typical farm wagon *c.* 1914. (SC.)

KELLEY BOULEVARD, 1912. The rural nature of Attleborough and its roads can be seen here. Travel on dirt roads could be an adventure during rainy, snowy, or muddy days. (SC.)

SNOW SCENE, C. 1885. Pictured is the South Main Street railroad crossing near Pearce and Carpenter Streets. The charm of this scene belies the difficulty of getting about during New England winters. Then, as now, snow can make travel difficult, whether its by horse-drawn vehicle or modern-day transportation. (SC.)

WINTER, 1880s. Posing on the Boston-Providence Railroad tracks, this group seems to enjoy the aftermath of a wind-driven snowstorm. The scene is north of Park Street, looking south. (SC.)

PARK STREET CROSSING, C. 1880s. Roaring through town, the railroad opened Attleborough's market to a larger world. Despite noise, pollution, and other inconveniences, the railroad was the key to a prosperous and growing community. The railroad made travel to and from the key cities of Boston and New York possible. (SC.)

MILL STREET CROSSING, 1902. With factories located near the main line and with branch lines throughout the town, the railroad moved not only people, but brought needed goods to and from the town. (SC.)

SOUTH MAIN STREET CROSSING, 1902. Warning signs and crossing gates offered warning of oncoming trains. Despite these attempts to avoid trouble, accidents were a constant danger and an all too familiar occurrence. (SC.)

ATTLEBORO ENGINE, C. 1912. These banners were hung over the street as warnings about a train engine's danger. (APL.)

TRAIN ON THE TRACKS! With the crossing gates down, people could see the approaching engine. This particular location is near that shown in the photograph at the top of page 94 but on a less wintry day. (APL, gift of Mrs. Gertrude Low.)

FREIGHT DEPOT. The moving of freight made the railroad important for Attleboro's industries. The undated photograph, looking northeast, shows the heavy traffic at the Attleboro freight depot. (SC.)

BUILDING THE ARCHES, 1906. A major railroad project to make the railroad's passage through Attleborough safer and faster was completed in 1906 with the elevation of the railroad tracks. A crew is seen here working on the South Main Street section of the project. (SC.)

OLIVE STREET BRIDGE. Railroad safety also included elimination of railroad street crossings by elevating some roads over the railroad tracks, as seen here with the construction of the Olive Street Bridge. Note the train on the left. (SC.)

BUILDING THE PARK STREET ARCHES. The amount of engineering skill and labor needed to elevate the tracks through the busy town center can perhaps be appreciated from this picture. With stone building materials visible at right, the project appears to be watched over by the twin churches of the Second Congregational Church. (SC.)

ARCHES COMPLETED. Traffic could now travel safely under the arches as trains came and went overhead. This photograph showing the passage of a train has a bit of mystery to it. Is the smoke coming from a Park Street fire? If so, which one? Or is the smoke from the locomotive itself? You decide. (SC.)

OLD DEPOT, C. 1904. Few photographs offer such a feast for the eyes. A water tower, people, horse and wagon, windmill, churches, and train, etc. The depot shown here would be replaced by another station farther down the track once the tracks were elevated. (APL.)

WORKERS. Attleboro's depot platform, Boston side, is the location where this group of railroad employees and workers paused for a photograph. (SC.)

CRASH! In spite of concerns for safety, railroad accidents were all too frequent. This photograph of car damage was taken on July 26, 1893. (APL, given by Mrs. Alice Potter.)

LOOKING NORTH. This photograph, taken from the Olive Street Bridge, looks north towards the center of Attleboro and shows the extensive railroad tracks within the city. (SC.)

WAITING FOR THE TROLLEY. Shorter trips to nearby towns, amusement parks, or casinos could be taken by trolley cars, like the one seen approaching from the right. The sign proclaims "Chicago" even though it is still in Attleboro. trolley car can be seen approaching on the right. (APL, gift of C. Gertrude Low.)

TROLLEY CAR AND WORKERS. Street railroad conductors and workers pause for a photograph in front of an electric trolley car. The first electric street railway was started in 1887 and ran between Attleborough and North Attleborough to Plainville. (SC.)

COUNTY STREETCAR. Trolley car workers and a child are shown here. Trolleys would run until 1932 in Attleboro; their decline began after WW I another, soon to be more popular, means of "getting about" gained riders: the automobile. (AHC.)

THE FLAMING YOUTH. This 1914 "Hot Rod" shows that automobile would soon become much more than a way of travel. (SC.)

POND STREET, 1922. As automobiles increased in both popularity and numbers, the need to improve streets became all too apparent. This task would fall to the City Department of Public Works, which was responsible for paving Attleboro's many miles of streets in the early 1920s. (DPW Album, AHC.)

PLEASANT STREET, 1921. The railroad ridge overhead may look much the same today, but the trolley tracks are gone, perhaps under the road, and the road itself is much improved. (DPW Album, AHC.)

HERRICKS CORNER, 1908. The scene shows Attleborough's leading department store, San Souci, with cars parked along Park Street. John Nerney would open the first automobile dealership in the town in 1903. A single-cylinder, air-cooled Cameron, made in nearby

Pawtucket, was the first car sold in Attleborough on February 22. Was it perhaps a President's Day Sale? (SC.)

MONUMENT SQUARE, 1921. DPW workers are seen here surfacing Monument Square. The grand monument, since removed to Capron Park, is seen behind the automobile on the right. (DPW Album, AHC.)

Eight
CELEBRATION
AND CEREMONIES

A town's celebration, ceremonies, and social events can tell much about the community and about life at that moment in time. Attleboro has had its share of such gatherings throughout the years. The following pictures show Attleboro as it celebrated various events and occasions.

SUMMER GATHERING. As in most New England cities and towns, Attleborough did its duty to help save the Union during the Civil War (1861–1865). Some 490 men from Attleborough enlisted in the military during the conflict and those left behind worked in local factories to produce cloth, buttons, buckles, and medals to help in the war effort. Shown here in 1912, survivors of the conflict are pictured lined up across the Bank and Park Streets intersection looking north. (SC.)

STANDING TALL, 1912. Showing signs of age, Grand Army of the Republic (GAR) members stand proudly for this gathering. Attleboro's GAR group was named in honor of William A. Streeter, who was killed on August 16, 1864, at the Battle of Deep Run in Virginia. (SC.)

CHANGING AGE, 1912. Still proudly wearing their uniforms and medals earned so long ago are members of the GAR group. Gatherings such as these, especially on Memorial Day, would keep the memory of the "War to Save the Union" alive for many years after the end of the hostilities. Members founded a GAR dining club in 1923, which held monthly dinners and continued to keep the memories of the war alive. The old GAR building on County Street would be torn down in 1963 to make way for a fountain and garden on the L.G. Balfour Co. property. (SC.)

IN FRONT OF THE YMCA. This photograph includes not only GAR veterans but also "Sons of Union" veterans. In 1971, Charles E. Hayward was able to identify many of those in the photograph. The identification can be found in the Attleboro Historical Commission files. (AHC, gift of Albert T. Gernner.)

DEDICATION CELEBRATION, 1908. The unveiling of Attleborough's Civil War Monument drew hundreds to what came to be known as Monument Square on Park Street. (SC.)

CIVIL WAR MONUMENT. Designed by "White of Quincy" and made of Quincy granite, the monument has three large, bronze military figures, which were molded at the Ames Foundry in Chicopee, Massachusetts. (AHC.)

MONUMENT SQUARE, 1908. Now located in Capron Park, Attleboro's Civil War Monument is atop a small rise that is seldom seen or considered by the motorists who pass by on busy County Street (SC.)

CROWD AT MONUMENT SQUARE COMMON. With Holman Street in the background, this early 1900s photograph shows a large gathering of people who have come by bicycle, horse-drawn carriage, or on foot to the festivities. (SC.)

ATTLEBOROUGH BAND. No celebration would be complete without music, and Attleboro has had numerous bands throughout the years to perform for such occasions. This early 1900 group poses in a cemetery as children look on. (SC.)

"OLD HOME WEEK," 1907. This popular event of the early 1900s, Old Home Week celebrations were held throughout New England including Attleboro. The crowd shown here at the railroad depot awaits the return of Attleboro's native sons and daughters and other visitors to the town's celebration. In the 1907 celebration from July 28 to August 3, Attleboro billed itself as the "M'F'G Jewelry Centre of America." Mitchell Mannering said that "those coming back to Attleboro's Old Home Week [would] feel that their own home [town] is a veritable jewel in itself." (AHC.)

COME ON BACK. Banners across Park Street announce the upcoming "Old Home Week" celebration, probably in 1907. (SC.)

PARK STREET CELEBRATION. Most of the town's celebrations were held in the center of town in and around what became Monument Square. It is now called Gilbert Perry Square and is located near the Common. This photograph shows the crowd during the Country Circus Parade (1906) or an Old Home Week celebration, possibly 1907. (SC.)

OFFICER GAFFNEY. Field and sporting events were usually included as part of the town's celebrations. This *c.* 1912 photograph was taken at Brady Field, Attleboro's most important field for such events. (SC.)

BRADY FIELD, C. 1912. Go! Boys enjoying a sprint as moms, dads, friends, and officer Gaffney look on. (SC.)

BRADY FIELD, C. 1912. Note the sign. It appears to read as follows: "You must say, are you the moose carnival girl for the $5 prizes?" (SC.)

COUNTY STREET AT NORTH MAIN STREETS. A trolley waits for a passing float to pass by during an early 1900s parade. (AHC, given by G. Lowell Brown.)

READY FOR OLD HOME WEEK, C. 1907. Businesses, like E.A. Wales, Jeweler, also participated in the town's celebration with the American flag and bunting as popular decorations. (SC.)

PRESIDENTIAL VISIT, APRIL 29, 1912. Pres. William Howard Taft would lose the election of 1912, but his visit to Attleboro drew a large gathering of people to the Attleboro Depot to hear and see him. (SC.)

ELECTION OF 1912. The watershed election of 1912 was also hotly debated in Attleboro as TR's Progressive Party's banner hangs at the corner of Park and South Main Streets. Another banner, just before the arches, further shows Attleboro's interest in the election. (SC.)

AN APPROACHING PARADE, 1913. With businesses decorated in patriotic bunting, people flocked to Park Street for the parade, possibly as part of an "Old Home Week" celebration. Taunton took advantage of an anticipated large audience to advertise its own 1914 celebration. (SC.)

PARK STREET PARADE, 1913. With bands and fraternal orders marching down Park Street, the crowd's patience is rewarded. (SC.)

BRADY FIELD IN ACTION, JUNE 1, 1912. Baseball rivalry between North Attleborough and Attleboro reached legendary proportions at Brady Field, where both towns would hire major league players to play for "their" town's team. Crowds from 8 to 9,000 showed up to watch the games and see big-league stars such as Babe Ruth, Grover Alexander, Rogers Hornsby, George

Sisler, "Rabbitt" Maranville, or Frankie Frisch, in what has come to be known as "The Little World Series." In 1921, former Mayor Harold E. Sweet and other sports-minded people donated land for a new field — Hayward Field—which, at the time, was considered one of the best ball parks in New England. Brady Field would fade into memory. (SC.)

RETURN OF THE CLOCK, 1929–1930. Some celebrations involving Attleboro took place elsewhere. When Edmund H. Gingras purchased an old clock at an East Mansfield auction, plans for such a celebration would be set in motion. Inside the clock's back cover was the following inscription: "U.S.S. Ethan Allen on blockade January 10, 1863." With the help of George E. Nerney, the GAR Dining Club, the U.S. Navy Department, and the Brunswick (Georgia) News, the clock's story was determined. The clock had been taken from an abandoned plantation house on Saint Simons Island, off the coast of Georgia and it needed to be returned to its rightful home. (AHC, photograph album and GAR Dining Club pamphlet.)

ON TO GEORGIA. Mayor Fred E. Briggs would head the Attleboro delegation to return the clock to Georgia. F.F. Blackington, William Nerney, Francis J. O'Neil, A.J. Laliberte, Postmaster J.V. Curran, E.H. Gingras, Roy Inman, C.C. Cain Jr., and Mr. and Mrs. Harry R. Holbrook made up the rest of the Attleboro delegation to Georgia. (AHC, photograph album and GAR Dining Club pamphlet.)

HOME AT LAST. Speaker of the day was Massachusetts Congressman Joseph W. Martin Jr. (right of the clock). Georgia Senator Walter F. George was designated as the speaker to receive the clock. All of Georgia joined in the celebration. (AHC, photograph album and GAR Dining Club pamphlet.)

OUTSIDE OF THE KING PLANTATION, CONGRESSMAN MARTIN'S RETURNING SPEECH WAS GREETED WITH MUCH APPLAUSE. Both Northern and Southern press praised Attleboro's "graceful act of courtesy." (AHC, photograph album and GAR Dining Club pamphlet.)

CAMPAIGNING. Thousands of people were attracted to Attleboro in 1940 as the presidential motorcade of Wendell L. Willkie moved slowly through Attleboro en route to Providence,

Rhode Island. Congressman Joseph W. Martin is right of Willkie. (AHC.)

ACKNOWLEDGMENTS

We would like to thank the many people who have helped us complete this book. Special thanks go to Marion Wrightington and Dyanne Spatcher, who gave generously of their time and knowledge to help us. Sincere appreciation goes to Mayor Judith Robbins for making access to the Attleboro Historical Commission's considerable files possible. We acknowledge the staff of the Attleboro Public Library, especially its research personnel, who were all most helpful.

More information about Attleboro can be found in some of the works that we consulted, including John Daggett's *Sketch of the History of Attleborough*, A. Irvin Studley's *History of Attleboro*, Paul H. Tedesco's *1894 Attleborough–Attleboro 1978*, and the *Attleboro Sun-Chronicle*.

The pictures used in this book come from three places: the files of the Attleboro Historical Commission (AHC); Attleboro Public Library (APL); and the Frank R. Sweet Memorial Collection of Photographs which is housed at the Attleboro Public Library (SC).